EMMANUEL JOSEPH

Godly Goals, Instilling Faith and Morality in Young Business Minds

Copyright © 2025 by Emmanuel Joseph

All rights reserved. No part of this publication may be reproduced, stored or transmitted in any form or by any means, electronic, mechanical, photocopying, recording, scanning, or otherwise without written permission from the publisher. It is illegal to copy this book, post it to a website, or distribute it by any other means without permission.

First edition

*This book was professionally typeset on Reedsy.
Find out more at reedsy.com*

Contents

1	Chapter 1: The Foundation of Godly Goals	1
2	Chapter 2: The Power of Vision and Faith	3
3	Chapter 3: Integrity in Business	5
4	Chapter 4: The Role of Compassion in Leadership	7
5	Chapter 5: Building a Business with Purpose	9
6	Chapter 6: The Power of Networking and Collaboration	11
7	Chapter 7: The Role of Resilience and Perseverance	13
8	Chapter 8: The Impact of Ethical Marketing	15
9	Chapter 9: The Power of Innovation	17
10	Chapter 10: The Importance of Work-Life Balance	19
11	Chapter 11: The Role of Mentorship and Guidance	21
12	Chapter 12: The Impact of Social Responsibility	23
13	Chapter 13: The Power of Faith in Overcoming Adversity	25
14	Chapter 14: The Importance of Continuous Learning	27
15	Chapter 15: Leaving a Legacy	29
16	Epilogue: The Journey Continues	31

1

Chapter 1: The Foundation of Godly Goals

In a bustling city where business thrives and ambition runs high, there lived a young entrepreneur named David. David's life was a testament to perseverance. Raised in a family that valued faith and moral integrity, he understood the importance of grounding his business ambitions in ethical principles. This chapter delves into the essential qualities that form the bedrock of godly goals and how young minds can align their aspirations with divine principles.

David's journey began when he decided to start a small tech company that focused on creating innovative solutions to everyday problems. Unlike many of his peers, David was determined to uphold his faith and moral values in every aspect of his business. He believed that success wasn't merely measured by profit but by the positive impact his company could make on society. His story serves as an inspiration for young entrepreneurs to build their dreams on a foundation of faith and morality.

As David's company grew, he faced numerous challenges that tested his principles. From dealing with dishonest competitors to making tough financial decisions, his faith became his guiding light. He often found solace in prayer, seeking wisdom and strength to navigate the tumultuous business world. This chapter emphasizes the importance of having a strong spiritual foundation and how it can help young business minds stay true to their values.

Moreover, this chapter explores the significance of setting godly goals that go beyond material success. David's vision wasn't just about creating a profitable business; it was about making a difference in the lives of others. He aimed to provide employment opportunities, support charitable causes, and contribute to the betterment of his community. His story highlights the importance of having a higher purpose and how it can lead to a more fulfilling and meaningful entrepreneurial journey.

In conclusion, the foundation of godly goals lies in the alignment of one's ambitions with faith and moral values. David's story illustrates that success is not just about achieving financial prosperity but about making a positive impact on the world. Young entrepreneurs can draw inspiration from his journey and strive to build their dreams on a foundation of faith, integrity, and purpose.

2

Chapter 2: The Power of Vision and Faith

A few years into his entrepreneurial journey, David met Sarah, an equally ambitious and faith-driven young woman. Sarah had a vision of starting an eco-friendly fashion brand that promoted sustainability and ethical practices. Together, they embarked on a mission to turn their dreams into reality, driven by a shared belief in the power of vision and faith.

Sarah's passion for sustainable fashion stemmed from her childhood experiences growing up in a small village where people lived in harmony with nature. She witnessed firsthand the devastating effects of environmental degradation and was determined to make a difference. Her unwavering faith in God and her vision for a better world fueled her entrepreneurial spirit. This chapter delves into the importance of having a clear vision and the role of faith in turning that vision into reality.

David and Sarah's partnership was built on a foundation of mutual respect, trust, and shared values. They believed that with faith, all things were possible, and their combined efforts could bring about positive change. Their journey was not without obstacles, but their faith kept them grounded and motivated. They often reminded each other of their higher purpose and the impact they wanted to make on the world. This chapter highlights the importance of having a strong support system and how faith can strengthen partnerships.

As their businesses grew, David and Sarah faced numerous challenges that tested their resolve. From managing limited resources to dealing with skeptical investors, they relied on their faith to persevere. They often turned to scripture for guidance and found inspiration in the stories of biblical figures who overcame adversity through unwavering faith. This chapter explores how young entrepreneurs can draw strength from their faith to overcome obstacles and stay focused on their goals.

Moreover, this chapter emphasizes the significance of setting long-term goals that align with one's vision and faith. David and Sarah's success wasn't just about achieving short-term milestones; it was about staying true to their values and making a lasting impact. Their story serves as a reminder that true success is measured not by financial gains but by the positive change one brings to the world.

In conclusion, the power of vision and faith is a driving force behind the success of young entrepreneurs. David and Sarah's journey illustrates that with a clear vision and unwavering faith, one can overcome challenges and achieve great things. Young business minds can draw inspiration from their story and strive to turn their dreams into reality, guided by faith and a higher purpose.

3

Chapter 3: Integrity in Business

David and Sarah's commitment to integrity became the cornerstone of their business endeavors. They understood that in a world where shortcuts and unethical practices were often rewarded, staying true to their moral values was paramount. This chapter delves into the importance of integrity in business and how young entrepreneurs can navigate the challenges of maintaining ethical standards.

Early in their journey, David and Sarah encountered numerous temptations to compromise their values for the sake of profit. From opportunities to cut corners in production to offers from shady investors, they faced constant pressure to deviate from their principles. However, their unwavering commitment to integrity guided their decisions. This chapter highlights the importance of having a moral compass and how it can help young entrepreneurs stay on the right path.

One of the defining moments in David and Sarah's journey was when they were offered a lucrative deal that required them to compromise their ethical standards. The pressure was immense, but they chose to stay true to their values, even if it meant losing the deal. Their decision was met with skepticism and criticism, but their integrity remained intact. This story serves as a powerful reminder that true success is not measured by financial gain but by the strength of one's character.

Moreover, this chapter explores the impact of integrity on building trust and credibility. David and Sarah's commitment to ethical practices earned them the respect and trust of their customers, employees, and partners. Their reputation for honesty and fairness became a valuable asset, attracting like-minded individuals and organizations to collaborate with them. This chapter emphasizes the long-term benefits of maintaining integrity in business and how it can lead to sustainable success.

In addition, this chapter discusses the role of integrity in creating a positive work culture. David and Sarah's commitment to ethical practices extended to how they treated their employees. They fostered an environment of transparency, respect, and accountability, which contributed to a motivated and loyal workforce. Their story highlights the importance of leading by example and how young entrepreneurs can create a positive impact on their teams through integrity.

In conclusion, integrity is a fundamental principle that young entrepreneurs must uphold in their business endeavors. David and Sarah's story illustrates that staying true to one's moral values can lead to lasting success and build a reputation of trust and credibility. By maintaining integrity, young business minds can navigate the challenges of the entrepreneurial journey and create a positive impact on the world.

4

Chapter 4: The Role of Compassion in Leadership

As David and Sarah's businesses grew, they realized the importance of compassionate leadership. They understood that true leadership wasn't just about making decisions and driving results; it was about caring for their teams and stakeholders. This chapter delves into the role of compassion in leadership and how young entrepreneurs can lead with empathy and kindness.

David's compassionate leadership was evident in how he treated his employees. He believed that a happy and motivated workforce was essential for the success of his company. He took the time to understand the needs and concerns of his team, creating a supportive and inclusive work environment. This chapter highlights the importance of leading with empathy and how it can foster a positive and productive work culture.

Similarly, Sarah's leadership style was characterized by her genuine care for her employees and customers. She often went above and beyond to ensure that her team felt valued and appreciated. Her compassion extended to her customers, as she prioritized their needs and feedback in her business decisions. This chapter explores how compassionate leadership can build strong relationships and create a loyal customer base.

Moreover, this chapter discusses the impact of compassion on decision-making. David and Sarah often faced difficult decisions that required balancing business objectives with ethical considerations. Their compassionate approach ensured that their decisions were guided by fairness and empathy. This chapter emphasizes the importance of considering the human aspect in business decisions and how it can lead to more sustainable and ethical outcomes.

In addition, this chapter highlights the significance of giving back to the community. David and Sarah's commitment to compassion extended beyond their businesses. They actively supported charitable causes and engaged in community initiatives. Their story serves as a reminder that true leadership involves making a positive impact on society. This chapter encourages young entrepreneurs to incorporate compassion into their leadership approach and contribute to the greater good.

In conclusion, compassion is a vital aspect of effective leadership. David and Sarah's story illustrates that leading with empathy and kindness can create a positive work culture, build strong relationships, and make a meaningful impact on society. Young business minds can draw inspiration from their journey and strive to lead with compassion in their entrepreneurial endeavors.

5

Chapter 5: Building a Business with Purpose

David and Sarah's entrepreneurial journey was driven by a deep sense of purpose. They understood that a successful business wasn't just about making money; it was about making a difference. This chapter delves into the importance of building a business with purpose and how young entrepreneurs can create ventures that align with their values and contribute to the greater good.

David's tech company was founded on the principle of creating innovative solutions that addressed real-world problems. He believed that technology had the power to improve lives and create positive change. This chapter explores how having a clear purpose can guide business decisions and inspire young entrepreneurs to pursue meaningful goals.

Similarly, Sarah's eco-friendly fashion brand was born out of her passion for sustainability and ethical practices. She was determined to create a brand that not only offered stylish and sustainable products but also promoted environmental awareness. This chapter highlights the importance of aligning business goals with personal values and how it can lead to a more fulfilling entrepreneurial journey.

Moreover, this chapter discusses the significance of setting long-term goals that reflect one's purpose. David and Sarah's success was not just measured by financial milestones but by the positive impact they made on the environment. Their dedication to sustainability and ethical practices became a core aspect of their businesses, influencing everything from product development to marketing strategies. This chapter emphasizes the importance of having a long-term vision and how it can guide young entrepreneurs in building businesses with purpose.

In addition, this chapter explores the benefits of having a purpose-driven business. David and Sarah's commitment to their values not only attracted like-minded customers but also inspired their employees. Their sense of purpose created a strong sense of community and loyalty within their teams. This chapter encourages young entrepreneurs to identify their purpose and use it as a driving force in their entrepreneurial journey.

In conclusion, building a business with purpose is essential for creating lasting success and making a positive impact on the world. David and Sarah's story illustrates that aligning business goals with personal values can lead to a more fulfilling and meaningful entrepreneurial journey. Young business minds can draw inspiration from their journey and strive to create ventures that reflect their purpose and contribute to the greater good.

6

Chapter 6: The Power of Networking and Collaboration

David and Sarah's journey taught them the importance of networking and collaboration. They understood that success in business often required the support and expertise of others. This chapter delves into the significance of building strong networks and collaborating with like-minded individuals and organizations.

David's tech company thrived on innovation, and he recognized the value of collaborating with other tech enthusiasts and professionals. He actively participated in industry events, joined tech forums, and built relationships with other entrepreneurs. This chapter highlights the benefits of networking and how it can open doors to new opportunities and insights.

Similarly, Sarah's eco-friendly fashion brand benefited from her collaboration with sustainable fashion advocates and environmental organizations. She believed that collective efforts were essential for creating meaningful change. Her partnerships with like-minded individuals and organizations allowed her to expand her reach and impact. This chapter explores how collaboration can enhance one's entrepreneurial journey and lead to greater success.

Moreover, this chapter discusses the importance of building a supportive network. David and Sarah's success was partly attributed to the mentors, advisors, and peers who guided and supported them along the way. They often sought advice from experienced professionals and valued the wisdom and insights they received. This chapter emphasizes the significance of having a strong support system and how it can contribute to one's growth and success.

In addition, this chapter highlights the role of collaboration in fostering innovation. David and Sarah often collaborated with others to bring fresh perspectives and ideas to their businesses. Their willingness to work with others allowed them to stay ahead of the curve and continuously innovate. This chapter encourages young entrepreneurs to embrace collaboration and leverage the power of collective efforts.

In conclusion, networking and collaboration are essential for achieving success in business. David and Sarah's story illustrates the importance of building strong networks and collaborating with like-minded individuals and organizations. Young business minds can draw inspiration from their journey and strive to build supportive networks and partnerships that enhance their entrepreneurial endeavors.

7

Chapter 7: The Role of Resilience and Perseverance

David and Sarah's entrepreneurial journey was marked by numerous challenges and setbacks. They understood that resilience and perseverance were key to overcoming obstacles and achieving success. This chapter delves into the importance of resilience and how young entrepreneurs can develop the strength to persevere in the face of adversity.

David's tech company faced several financial challenges in its early stages. From securing funding to managing cash flow, he encountered numerous obstacles that tested his resolve. However, his unwavering faith and determination kept him going. This chapter explores how resilience can help young entrepreneurs navigate the ups and downs of the business world and stay focused on their goals.

Similarly, Sarah's eco-friendly fashion brand faced its share of challenges. From sourcing sustainable materials to gaining market acceptance, she encountered numerous hurdles that required perseverance. Her passion for sustainability and her faith in her vision gave her the strength to keep pushing forward. This chapter highlights the importance of having a strong sense of purpose and how it can fuel resilience.

Moreover, this chapter discusses the role of mindset in developing resilience. David and Sarah often faced situations that required them to adapt and learn from their mistakes. Their growth mindset allowed them to view challenges as opportunities for learning and improvement. This chapter emphasizes the importance of having a positive and growth-oriented mindset and how it can contribute to resilience.

In addition, this chapter highlights the significance of seeking support during challenging times. David and Sarah often turned to their faith, mentors, and support networks for encouragement and guidance. Their story illustrates that seeking help and relying on a strong support system can provide the strength needed to persevere. This chapter encourages young entrepreneurs to build a support system that can help them stay resilient.

In conclusion, resilience and perseverance are essential qualities for achieving success in business. David and Sarah's story illustrates that with faith, determination, and a positive mindset, young entrepreneurs can overcome challenges and achieve their goals. Their journey serves as an inspiration for young business minds to stay resilient and persevere in the face of adversity.

8

Chapter 8: The Impact of Ethical Marketing

David and Sarah's businesses thrived not only because of their innovative products but also because of their ethical marketing practices. They understood that building trust with their customers required honesty and transparency. This chapter delves into the importance of ethical marketing and how young entrepreneurs can create authentic and trustworthy brands.

David's tech company was known for its innovative solutions, but it was their ethical marketing that truly set them apart. David believed in being transparent with his customers about the benefits and limitations of his products. This chapter explores how honesty and transparency can build trust and credibility with customers and create a loyal customer base.

Similarly, Sarah's eco-friendly fashion brand gained popularity because of its commitment to sustainability and ethical practices. She ensured that her marketing messages were aligned with her brand values and that her customers were well-informed about the environmental impact of their purchases. This chapter highlights the importance of aligning marketing strategies with ethical principles and how it can attract like-minded customers.

Moreover, this chapter discusses the role of storytelling in ethical marketing.

David and Sarah often shared their personal stories and the journeys behind their businesses with their customers. Their authenticity and genuine passion resonated with their audience, creating a strong emotional connection. This chapter emphasizes the power of storytelling in building authentic brands and fostering customer loyalty.

In addition, this chapter highlights the significance of social responsibility in marketing. David and Sarah's commitment to ethical practices extended to their marketing campaigns. They often promoted social and environmental causes and encouraged their customers to make a positive impact. This chapter explores how integrating social responsibility into marketing strategies can enhance a brand's reputation and attract conscious consumers.

In conclusion, ethical marketing is essential for building trust and credibility with customers. David and Sarah's story illustrates that honesty, transparency, and authenticity can create strong and loyal customer relationships. Young entrepreneurs can draw inspiration from their journey and strive to create ethical and trustworthy brands that resonate with their audience.

9

Chapter 9: The Power of Innovation

Innovation was at the heart of David and Sarah's entrepreneurial success. They understood that staying ahead in the business world required continuous creativity and innovation. This chapter delves into the importance of innovation and how young entrepreneurs can foster a culture of creativity in their ventures.

David's tech company was known for its groundbreaking solutions that addressed everyday problems. He believed that innovation was the key to staying competitive and relevant in the fast-paced tech industry. This chapter explores how young entrepreneurs can embrace innovation and continuously seek new ways to improve their products and services.

Similarly, Sarah's eco-friendly fashion brand thrived on its innovative designs and sustainable practices. She was constantly exploring new materials and production methods that minimized environmental impact. Her commitment to innovation allowed her brand to stand out in the crowded fashion market. This chapter highlights the importance of staying curious and open to new ideas and how it can lead to business growth.

Moreover, this chapter discusses the significance of fostering a culture of innovation within a team. David and Sarah encouraged their employees to think creatively and contribute new ideas. They believed that a collaborative and open-minded work environment was essential for innovation. This chapter emphasizes the importance of creating a supportive and inclusive culture that nurtures creativity.

In addition, this chapter explores the role of technology in driving innovation. David and Sarah leveraged the latest technological advancements to enhance their products and streamline their operations. Their willingness to embrace technology allowed them to stay ahead of the curve and continuously innovate. This chapter encourages young entrepreneurs to stay informed about technological trends and incorporate them into their businesses.

In conclusion, innovation is a driving force behind business success. David and Sarah's story illustrates that staying curious, open-minded, and committed to continuous improvement can lead to groundbreaking achievements. Young business minds can draw inspiration from their journey and strive to foster a culture of innovation in their entrepreneurial endeavors.

10

Chapter 10: The Importance of Work-Life Balance

As David and Sarah's businesses grew, they realized the importance of maintaining a healthy work-life balance. They understood that true success wasn't just about achieving business goals but also about nurturing their personal well-being. This chapter delves into the significance of work-life balance and how young entrepreneurs can achieve harmony in their professional and personal lives.

David's tech company demanded a significant amount of his time and energy. In the early stages of his business, he often found himself working long hours and neglecting his personal life. However, he soon realized that burnout was detrimental to both his health and his business. This chapter explores how young entrepreneurs can prioritize self-care and set boundaries to achieve a healthy work-life balance.

Similarly, Sarah's eco-friendly fashion brand required her to juggle multiple responsibilities. From designing new collections to managing operations, she often felt overwhelmed. However, she understood the importance of taking time for herself and nurturing her personal relationships. This chapter highlights the significance of self-care and how it can contribute to overall well-being and productivity.

Moreover, this chapter discusses the role of time management in achieving work-life balance. David and Sarah implemented effective time management strategies to ensure that they could meet their business objectives while also making time for their personal lives. This chapter emphasizes the importance of setting priorities and creating a balanced schedule that allows for both work and leisure.

In addition, this chapter explores the benefits of maintaining a healthy work-life balance. David and Sarah realized that maintaining a healthy work-life balance improved their overall well-being and productivity. They found that taking breaks and spending time with loved ones helped them recharge and stay motivated. Their story serves as a reminder that success in business should not come at the expense of personal health and happiness. This chapter encourages young entrepreneurs to prioritize work-life balance and create a harmonious lifestyle.

In conclusion, achieving a healthy work-life balance is essential for long-term success and well-being. David and Sarah's story illustrates that taking care of oneself and nurturing personal relationships can lead to a more fulfilling and productive entrepreneurial journey. Young business minds can draw inspiration from their journey and strive to create a balanced lifestyle that allows for both professional and personal growth.

11

Chapter 11: The Role of Mentorship and Guidance

David and Sarah's entrepreneurial journey was greatly influenced by the mentors and advisors who guided them along the way. They understood the importance of seeking wisdom and learning from the experiences of others. This chapter delves into the significance of mentorship and how young entrepreneurs can benefit from guidance and support.

David's first mentor was a seasoned entrepreneur named John, who had successfully built and sold several tech companies. John's insights and advice were invaluable to David as he navigated the complexities of the business world. This chapter explores the benefits of having a mentor and how their guidance can provide valuable perspectives and knowledge.

Similarly, Sarah was mentored by a renowned fashion designer named Emma, who shared her passion for sustainability. Emma's mentorship helped Sarah refine her designs and navigate the challenges of the fashion industry. This chapter highlights the importance of finding mentors who share similar values and goals and how their support can contribute to one's growth.

Moreover, this chapter discusses the role of mentorship in personal development. David and Sarah's mentors not only provided business advice but also helped them grow as individuals. Their mentors encouraged them to reflect on their values, strengths, and areas for improvement. This chapter emphasizes the significance of holistic mentorship that addresses both professional and personal development.

In addition, this chapter explores the importance of being open to feedback and learning from others. David and Sarah valued the constructive feedback they received from their mentors and peers. They understood that continuous learning and growth were essential for success. This chapter encourages young entrepreneurs to seek mentorship, be open to feedback, and continuously strive for improvement.

In conclusion, mentorship and guidance are invaluable for young entrepreneurs. David and Sarah's story illustrates that seeking wisdom from experienced individuals can provide valuable insights and support. Young business minds can draw inspiration from their journey and seek mentors who can guide them in their entrepreneurial endeavors.

12

Chapter 12: The Impact of Social Responsibility

David and Sarah's commitment to social responsibility became a defining aspect of their businesses. They understood that businesses had a role to play in creating a positive impact on society. This chapter delves into the importance of social responsibility and how young entrepreneurs can integrate it into their ventures.

David's tech company was dedicated to using technology for social good. He believed that innovation should be used to address pressing societal issues, such as education and healthcare. This chapter explores how young entrepreneurs can identify social causes they are passionate about and create solutions that contribute to the greater good.

Similarly, Sarah's eco-friendly fashion brand was founded on the principle of promoting sustainability and environmental awareness. She actively engaged in initiatives that supported environmental conservation and education. This chapter highlights the significance of aligning business practices with social responsibility and how it can create a positive impact on society.

Moreover, this chapter discusses the benefits of social responsibility for businesses. David and Sarah's commitment to ethical practices and social causes earned them the trust and loyalty of their customers. Their dedication to making a positive impact became a unique selling point for their brands. This chapter emphasizes the importance of integrating social responsibility into business strategies and how it can enhance a brand's reputation.

In addition, this chapter explores the role of social responsibility in building strong communities. David and Sarah actively supported local initiatives and engaged with their communities. Their efforts contributed to creating a sense of belonging and solidarity. This chapter encourages young entrepreneurs to engage with their communities and contribute to social causes that resonate with their values.

In conclusion, social responsibility is essential for creating a positive impact on society and building a reputable brand. David and Sarah's story illustrates that aligning business practices with social causes can lead to meaningful and lasting success. Young business minds can draw inspiration from their journey and strive to integrate social responsibility into their entrepreneurial endeavors.

13

Chapter 13: The Power of Faith in Overcoming Adversity

David and Sarah's faith played a crucial role in helping them overcome adversity. They understood that challenges were inevitable in the entrepreneurial journey, and their faith provided them with the strength and resilience to persevere. This chapter delves into the power of faith in overcoming adversity and how young entrepreneurs can draw strength from their spiritual beliefs.

David's tech company faced a major setback when a critical project failed, resulting in significant financial losses. The situation was dire, and he felt overwhelmed by the pressure. However, his faith in God gave him the courage to keep going. He often turned to prayer for guidance and found solace in his spiritual beliefs. This chapter explores how faith can provide comfort and strength during difficult times.

Similarly, Sarah's eco-friendly fashion brand encountered challenges when a key supplier went out of business, disrupting their supply chain. The uncertainty was daunting, but Sarah's faith kept her grounded. She believed that God had a plan for her and trusted that things would work out. This chapter highlights the importance of having faith and how it can help young entrepreneurs stay hopeful and motivated.

Moreover, this chapter discusses the role of faith in finding meaning and purpose in adversity. David and Sarah often reflected on their challenges and found lessons in their experiences. Their faith helped them see adversity as an opportunity for growth and self-improvement. This chapter emphasizes the importance of maintaining a positive outlook and finding meaning in difficult situations.

In addition, this chapter explores the significance of community and support in overcoming adversity. David and Sarah's faith communities provided them with encouragement and support during tough times. Their story illustrates that having a strong support system can provide the strength needed to persevere. This chapter encourages young entrepreneurs to build a network of support and draw strength from their faith and community.

In conclusion, faith is a powerful source of strength and resilience in overcoming adversity. David and Sarah's story illustrates that with faith, young entrepreneurs can find comfort, meaning, and purpose in challenging situations. Their journey serves as an inspiration for young business minds to draw strength from their spiritual beliefs and stay resilient in the face of adversity.

14

Chapter 14: The Importance of Continuous Learning

David and Sarah's commitment to continuous learning was a key factor in their success. They understood that the business world was constantly evolving, and staying informed and adaptable was essential. This chapter delves into the importance of continuous learning and how young entrepreneurs can stay ahead in their industries.

David's tech company thrived on innovation, and he recognized the importance of staying updated with the latest technological advancements. He actively sought out learning opportunities, from attending industry conferences to enrolling in online courses. This chapter explores how young entrepreneurs can prioritize continuous learning and stay informed about industry trends.

Similarly, Sarah's eco-friendly fashion brand benefited from her commitment to learning about sustainable practices and materials. She regularly researched new developments in the field and sought advice from experts. Her dedication to continuous learning allowed her brand to stay competitive and relevant. This chapter highlights the importance of being curious and open to new knowledge and how it can lead to business growth.

Moreover, this chapter discusses the role of self-improvement in continuous learning. David and Sarah were committed to personal development and often engaged in activities that enhanced their skills and knowledge. This chapter emphasizes the significance of setting personal learning goals and actively seeking opportunities for growth.

In addition, this chapter explores the benefits of a learning-oriented mindset. David and Sarah's willingness to learn and adapt allowed them to navigate challenges and seize new opportunities. Their story illustrates that continuous learning can lead to innovation and success. This chapter encourages young entrepreneurs to adopt a learning-oriented mindset and prioritize ongoing education.

In conclusion, continuous learning is essential for staying competitive and achieving success in business. David and Sarah's story illustrates that staying informed and adaptable can lead to innovation and growth. Young business minds can draw inspiration from their journey and strive to prioritize continuous learning in their entrepreneurial endeavors.

15

Chapter 15: Leaving a Legacy

As David and Sarah's businesses flourished, they began to think about the legacy they wanted to leave behind. They understood that true success wasn't just about achieving financial milestones but about making a lasting impact on the world. This chapter delves into the importance of leaving a legacy and how young entrepreneurs can create a meaningful and enduring impact.

David's tech company had grown into a leading innovator in the industry, and he wanted to ensure that his work continued to make a positive impact even after he was gone. He established a foundation that supported technological education and innovation, providing opportunities for young minds to pursue their dreams. This chapter explores how young entrepreneurs can think beyond their immediate success and create a lasting legacy.

Similarly, Sarah's eco-friendly fashion brand had become a symbol of sustainability and ethical practices. She wanted her brand to continue promoting environmental awareness and inspiring others to make a difference. She created a mentorship program that supported aspiring sustainable fashion designers and entrepreneurs. This chapter highlights the importance of creating initiatives that can have a lasting and positive impact on society.

Moreover, this chapter discusses the role of values and principles in leaving a legacy. David and Sarah's commitment to their values guided their decisions and actions throughout their entrepreneurial journey. Their legacy was built on the principles of faith, integrity, compassion, and social responsibility. This chapter emphasizes the importance of staying true to one's values and how it can create a meaningful and enduring impact.

In addition, this chapter explores the significance of inspiring and empowering others. David and Sarah's journey inspired countless young entrepreneurs to pursue their dreams and make a positive impact on the world. Their story serves as a reminder that true success is measured not by personal achievements but by the lives one touches and the difference one makes. This chapter encourages young entrepreneurs to think about the legacy they want to leave and how they can inspire and empower others to continue their mission.

In conclusion, leaving a legacy is about creating a lasting and positive impact on the world. David and Sarah's story illustrates that true success is measured not by personal achievements but by the difference one makes in the lives of others. Young business minds can draw inspiration from their journey and strive to create meaningful and enduring legacies that reflect their values and contribute to the greater good.

16

Epilogue: The Journey Continues

David and Sarah's entrepreneurial journey was filled with challenges, triumphs, and valuable lessons. Their commitment to faith, integrity, compassion, and social responsibility guided them in building successful and impactful businesses. As they looked back on their journey, they felt a deep sense of fulfillment and gratitude for the experiences and opportunities they had encountered.

Their story serves as an inspiration for young entrepreneurs to pursue their dreams with faith and moral values. By setting godly goals and staying true to their principles, they can achieve success that goes beyond financial prosperity and makes a positive impact on the world. David and Sarah's legacy continues to inspire and empower the next generation of business minds to create meaningful and purposeful ventures.

As you embark on your own entrepreneurial journey, remember the lessons from David and Sarah's story. Stay grounded in your faith, uphold your values, and strive to make a difference. The journey may be challenging, but with resilience, perseverance, and a higher purpose, you can achieve great things and leave a lasting legacy.

Book Description: Godly Goals: Instilling Faith and Morality in Young Business Minds

Imagine a world where business isn't just about profits, but about making a positive impact. **"Godly Goals"** is an inspiring journey that follows two young entrepreneurs, David and Sarah, as they navigate the highs and lows of building their businesses while staying true to their faith and moral values.

David is a tech whiz who believes in using technology for good. Sarah is a fashion enthusiast committed to sustainability. Together, they show how success is not just about financial gain, but about integrity, compassion, and making a difference in the world.

Through their story, you'll learn about the importance of setting goals that align with your faith, staying resilient in the face of challenges, and leading with compassion. You'll see how ethical marketing can build trust and how continuous learning keeps you ahead in your industry.

"Godly Goals" is a heartfelt guide for young entrepreneurs who want to build businesses that reflect their values and leave a lasting legacy. It's about finding purpose, making a positive impact, and staying true to yourself every step of the way. Join David and Sarah on their journey and be inspired to pursue your own godly goals.

www.ingramcontent.com/pod-product-compliance
Lightning Source LLC
LaVergne TN
LVHW010442070526
838199LV00066B/6149